Clump-a-Dump and Snickle-Snack

Pentatonic Children's Songs

by Johanne Russ

MERCURY PRESS

Original Edition, Schwinge, Schwengel, Schwinge. Copyright 1966. Ultgeverij Vrij Geestesleven, Zeist-Holland Harmonielaan 7. Translated by Lyn S. Willwerth, with kind permission of Ultgeverij Vrij Geestesleven. American edition published by Kundry Willwerth.

ISBN 978-1-957569-11-6

MERCURY PRESS
an imprint of SteinerBooks
PO Box 58
Hudson, NY 12534

www.steinerbooks.org

Printed in the United States of America

Preface

These songs are published for the many children who love them already, having learned them from their teachers in Waldorf Kindergartens in USA. Now parents will have access to them in English translation and be able to join in singing with their children.

The fairy-tale content and holiday mood of the texts have made them particularly useful in rhythmic games and plays. The translations came about as needed in singing and playing with pre-school children. The melodies are composed in the pentatonic scale as Rudolf Steiner suggested for the young child.

Two songs, on pages 20 and 25, are translated by Ruth Hofrichter.

For the cover design and lovely drawings I want to thank Deborah Kaufman.

Summer 1977

Kundry Willwerth

Contents

Saddle My Pony

H. Diestel

Sad- - dle my po- - ny free
so it may car - ry me.
Neighs like a trum- pet blast,
runs like the wind so fast.
Sad- dle my po- - ny free,
so it may car- - ry me.
Lyre ostinato

Pinkepank

M. Garff

Lyre prelude
Hark what's com-ming, puff, puff, puff, that is Pin-ke-

-pank, the dwarf, 'neath the thorn-bush, by the lane,
stops to catch his breath a-gain, lifts his sack, and
tink-ling roll sil-ver, pre-cious stone and gold.
If you're spy-ing se-cret-ly
and, by chance, if he should see, quick, he packs them
one by one, sil-ver, gold and pre-cious stone,
back he takes them, lit-tle Knave, in the dark-ness
of his cave, and in vain you search the ground
for the pre-cious di-a-mond.
Lyre postlude
ostinato to the song

Softly, Softly, Softly Hark

H. Diestel

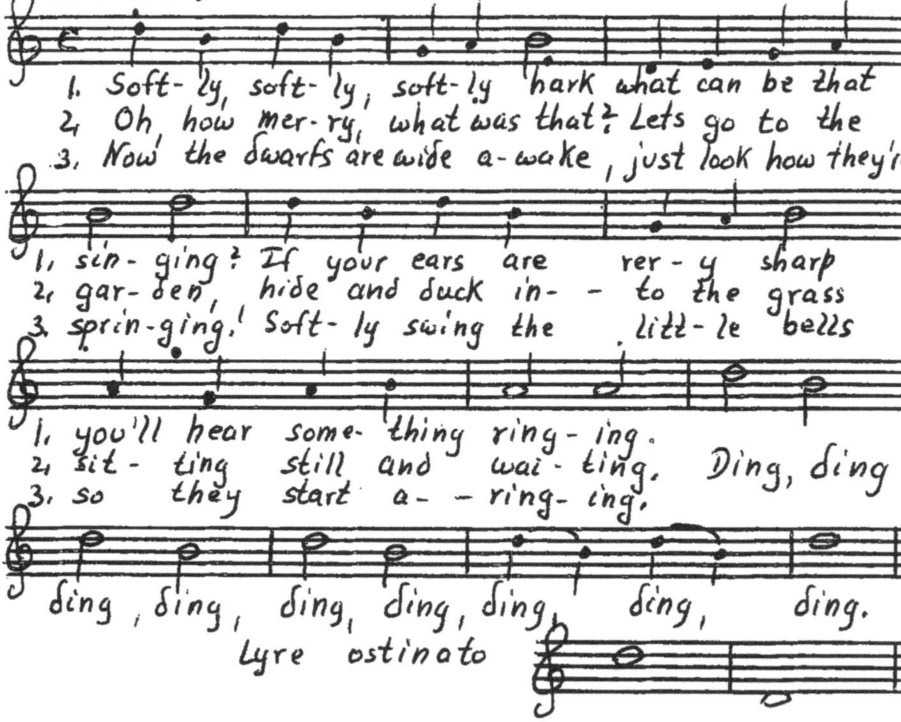
1. Soft- ly, soft- ly, soft- ly hark what can be that
2. Oh how mer- ry, what was that? Lets go to the
3. Now the dwarfs are wide a- wake, just look how they're
1. sin- ging? If your ears are ver- y sharp
2. gar- den, hide and duck in- - to the grass
3. sprin- ging! Soft- ly swing the litt- le bells
1. you'll hear some- thing ring- ing.
2. sit- ting still and wai- ting. Ding, ding
3. so they start a- - ring- ing.
ding, ding, ding, ding, ding, ding, ding.
Lyre ostinato

Swinging, Swinging

M. Garff

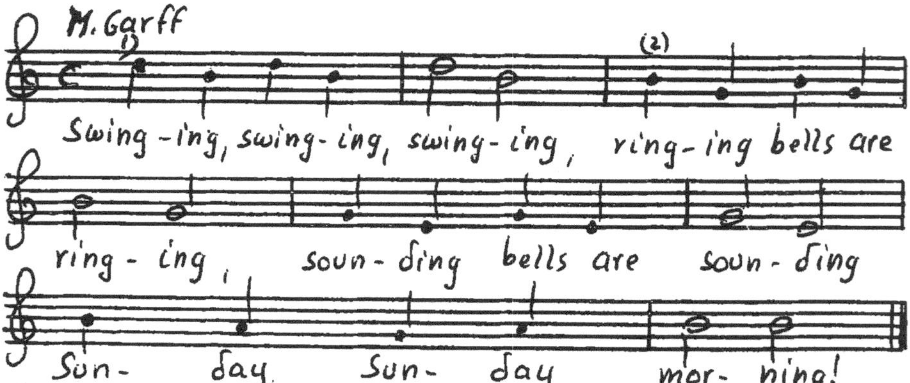
(1)
(2)
Swing- ing, swing- ing, swing- ing, ring- ing bells are
ring- ing, soun- ding bells are soun- ding
Sun- day, Sun- day mor- ning!

(Can be sung as a round.)

Bang, Bang, Bang

Lyre
Bang, bang, bang, the forge is glow-ing smi-thy take your ham-mer up,
Pan, pan, pan, le feu s'al-lu-me, for-ge-ron, prends ton mar-teau.
ham-mer, ham-mer on the an-vil strike the iron while it is hot.
Frap-pe, frap-pe sur l'en-clu-me, bats le fer quand il est chaud.
Bang, bang, bang, bang, bang, bang, bang, bang
Pan, pan, pan, pan, pan, pan, pan, pan
pan, pan, pan, pan, pan, pan, pan.

Clump-a-Dump & Snicklesnack

H. Diestel

Lyre prelude

1.-4. Clump- a - dump and Snick - le - snack
5. Stabs and grabs with hea - vy hand
6. Sticks his shag - gy head and all
7. With a grumb - le and a groan

1. go a- jour -ney right- ly, snea-King with their
2. feet, with care they set them, fea-ring that with
3. for their lives are run - ning, with their sacks u-
4. at the mountain stand they quick-ly in with
5. in the roots and bu - shes; shakes the mountain
6. in-to cliffs and boul-ders. Clum-sy fel- low
7. on the gi- ant wan-ders, rubs his shoul-der

1. sil- ver- sack on their tip-toes light- ly,
2. sack and pack Ne- ver - good might get them.
3. pon their backs how the wind is hum - ming.
4. sack and pack slip our dwarfs right han - dy.
5. and the land hea - vy stones he pu- shes.
6. stum-bles, falls down u- -pon his shoul- ders.
7. on a stone through the fo-rest blun- ders.

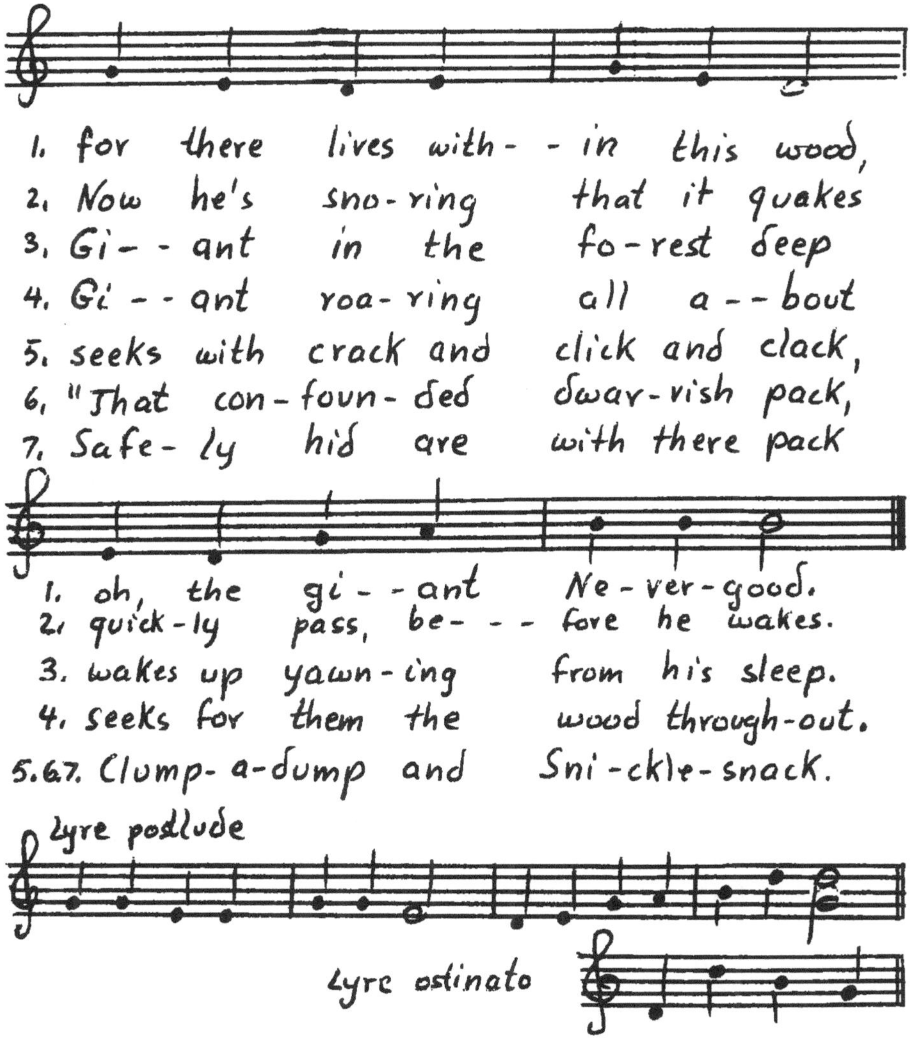
1. for there lives with- - in this wood,
2. Now he's sno-ring that it quakes
3. Gi- - ant in the fo-rest deep
4. Gi - - ant roa-ring all a- - bout
5. seeks with crack and click and clack,
6. "That con-foun-ded dwar-vish pack,
7. Safe-ly hid are with there pack
1. oh, the gi- - ant Ne-ver-good.
2. quick-ly pass, be- - - fore he wakes.
3. wakes up yawn-ing from his sleep.
4. seeks for them the wood through-out.
5.6.7. Clump-a-dump and Sni-ckle-snack.
Lyre postlude
Lyre ostinato

The Dwarfs' Day

H. Diestel

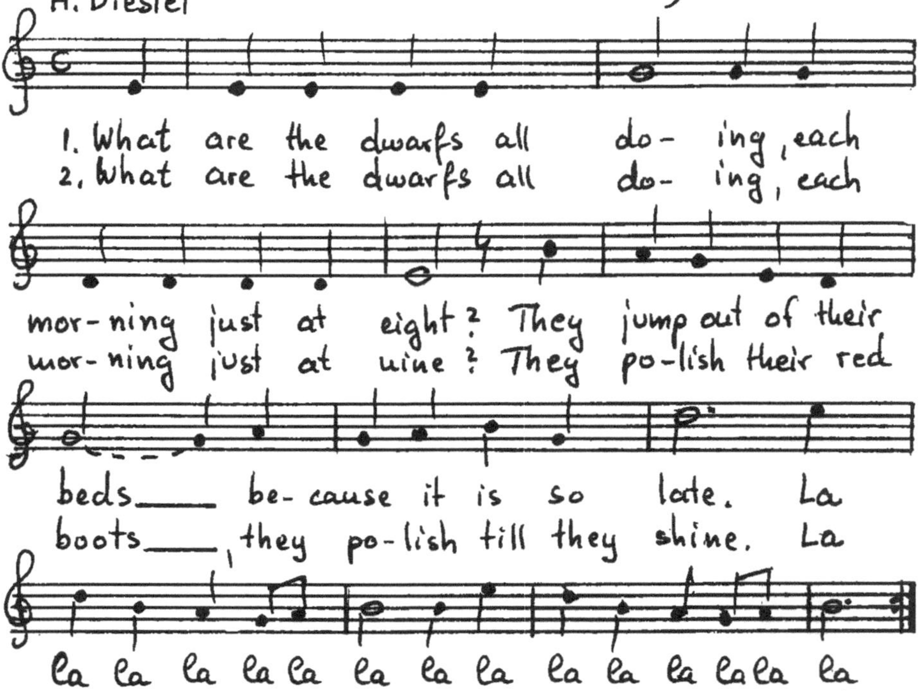
1. What are the dwarfs all do- ing, each mor-ning just at eight? They jump out of their beds___ be-cause it is so late. La
2. What are the dwarfs all do- ing, each mor-ning just at nine? They po-lish their red boots___, they po-lish till they shine. La
la la la la la la la la la la la lala la

What are the dwarfs all doing, each morning just at ten? They skip out to the meadow, they skip out to the glen. La la la ...

What are the dwarfs all doing, each morning just at eleven? They call up to the swallow, the swallow in the heaven. La la la ...

What are the dwarfs all doing, each morning just at twelve o'clock, at noon? They're sitting down to dinner and eating with their spoon. La.

What are the dwarfs all doing, each afternoon at one? They tiptoe past a bunny asleeping in the sun. La la la ...

What are the dwarfs all doing, each afternoon at two? They're wading through the puddles and wet is sock and shoe. La la la .....

What are the dwarfs all doing, each afternoon at three? They see a little squirrel and chase it up a tree. La la la ...

What are the dwarfs all doing, each afternoon at four? They clean their little cabin, they clean from roof to floor. La la la ...

What are the dwarfs all doing, each afternoon at five? They're hitching up their pony to go out for a drive. La la la ...

What are the dwarfs all doing, each afternoon at six? They build a fire for cooking, they build it out of sticks. La la la ...

What are the dwarfs all doing, each afternoon at seven? They bake their bread for supper, they bake it with good leven. La la la ...

What are the dwarfs all doing, each afternoon at eight? They all go in their cabin and then they shut the gate. La la la ...

Wee Dwarfs

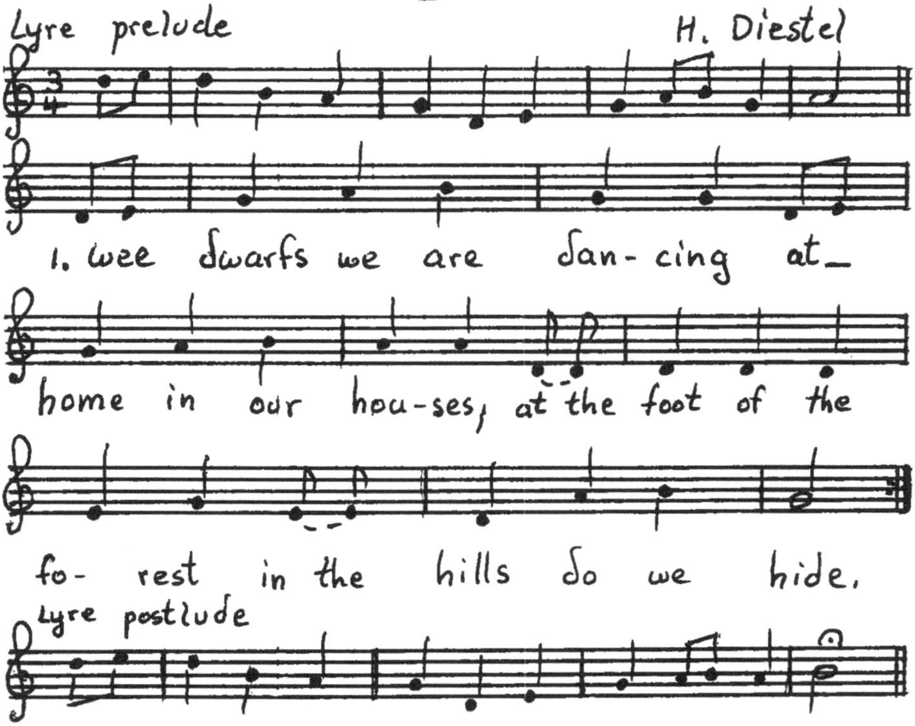
Lyre prelude
H. Diestel
1. Wee dwarfs we are dan- cing at_
home in our hou-ses, at the foot of the
fo- rest in the hills so we hide.
Lyre postlude

Anyone who would listen can hear us a-hamm'ring,
And mightily moving like folk at the forge.

Our bakers are baking the brown bread and biscuits;
They're beating the batter for rye-bread and rusks.

The smiths at their smithy are blowing the bellows
All rightly are rounding the rolling gold rings.

The weavers are weaving the wefts full of wonder
And sew with their silvery silk all their seams.

The cobblers are cobbling; they're sewing and stitching,

And hammering hard on the soles of our shoes.

But notice the night when the midnight is nearing,
The gates that are guarding the hall in the hill.

Then dwarfs drawing forth with their colorful coats
Their fools' caps they carry to party and feast.

We're dandling and dancing; we're hobliog and hopping
We clap and we clap with the music and moon.

But see how the sun rises high in the heaven
We hie us to hide in our hole in the hill.

Bird in the Tree

M. Garff

Lyre Prelude
Bird in the tree what song do you sing?
Ea-ster-tide dream___ to you I bring,
fly o-ver woods, o-ver the rye,
in- to the world, high-er, so high,
wing far a- - way___, for-tune so true___,
yet hap-pi - ly___ re - turn to you,
build me my nest high in the tree,

snugg-ly we rest___ my young and me."
"Bird in the tree what song do you sing?"
"Ea-ster-tide dream___ to you I bring."
Lyre postlude

Oh, My Soul

Round

Old Irish
(1)
(2)
Oh my soul__, oh my soul___ is in the
light of the moun - - tains. Arch-an-gel
Mi-cha-el stay my soul. Arch-an-gel
Mi-cha-el stay my soul.___ Mi-cha-el.
(2)
Ending
(1)
Lyre
14 times

Clip-de-clap

M. Garff

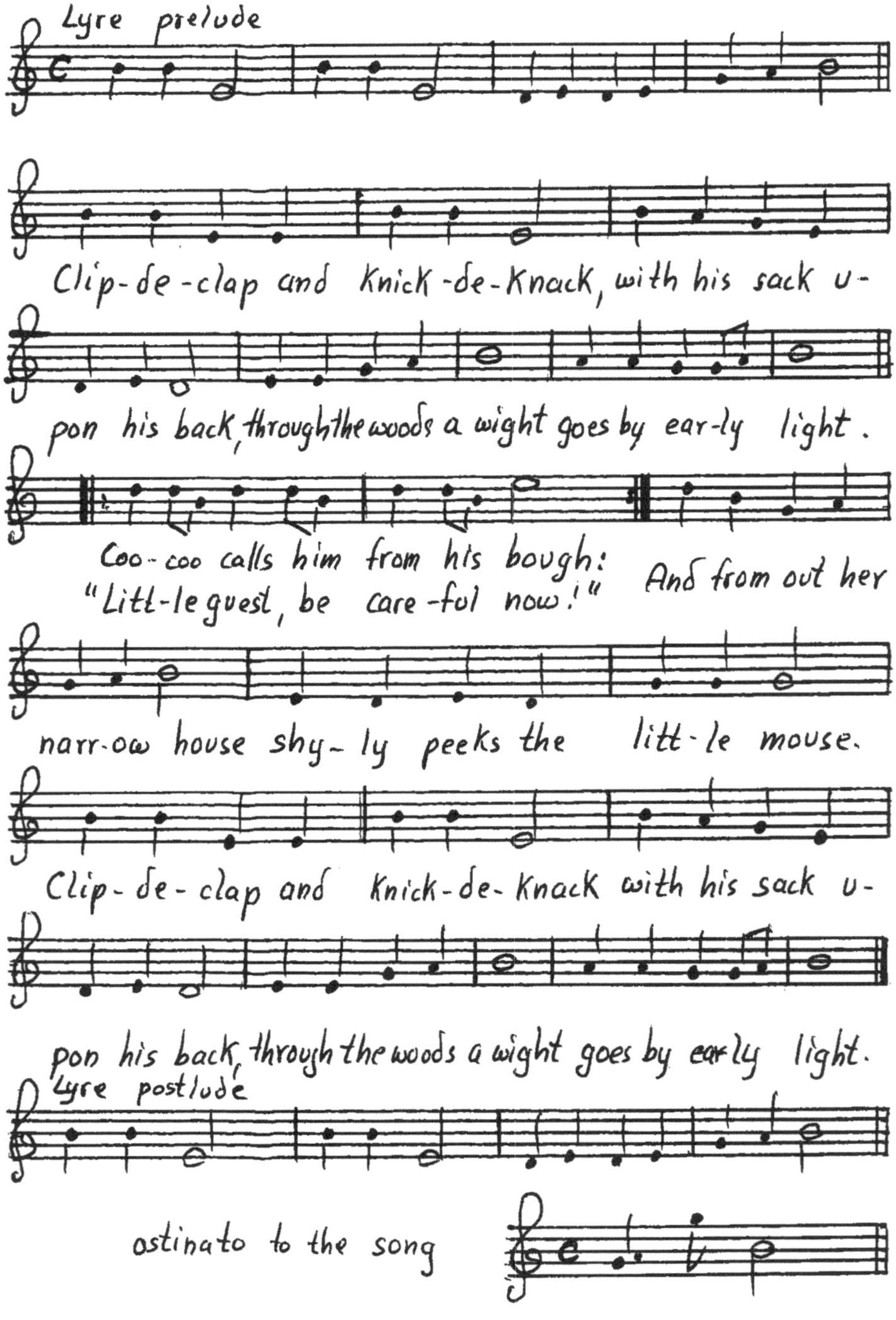
Lyre prelude
Clip-de-clap and Knick-de-Knack, with his sack u-
pon his back, through the woods a wight goes by ear-ly light.
Coo-coo calls him from his bough:
"Litt-le guest, be care-ful now!"
And from out her
narr-ow house shy-ly peeks the litt-le mouse.
Clip-de-clap and Knick-de-Knack with his sack u-
pon his back, through the woods a wight goes by early light.
Lyre postlude
ostinato to the song

When Mary goes walking

Patrick Chalmers

When Ma-ry goes wal-king, the
au-tumn winds blow, the pop-lars, they
curt-sey, the lar-ches bend low, the
oaks and the bee-ches their gold they fling
down, to make her a car-pet, to
make her a crown, to make her a
car-pet, to make her a crown.
Humm repeat.
(ostinato) Ending

It Snows

M. Garff

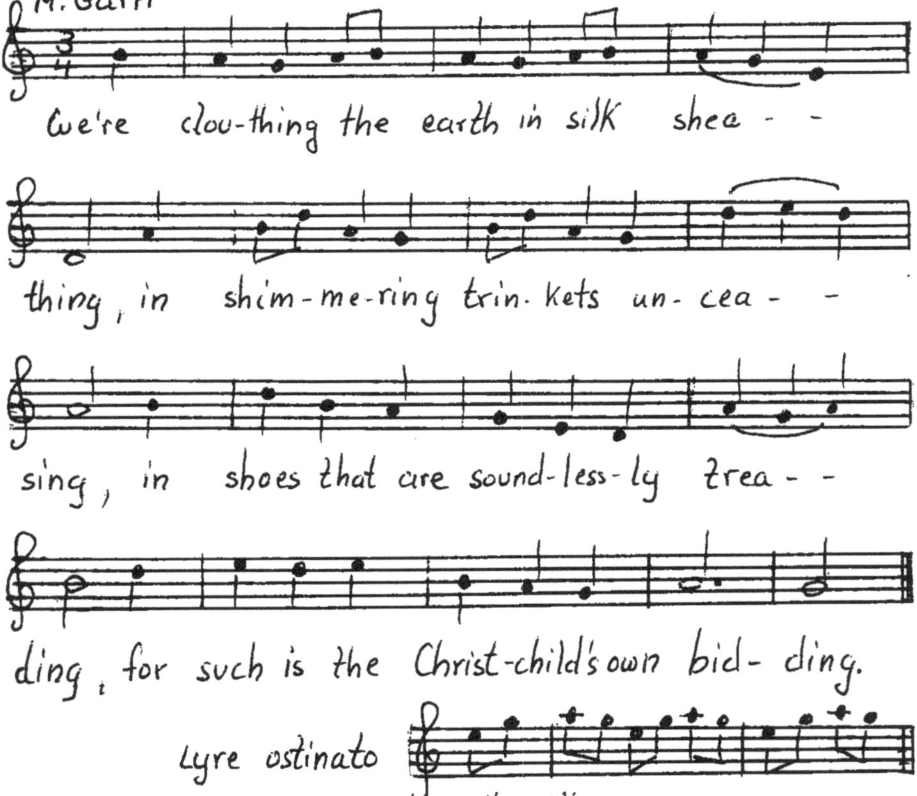
We're clou-thing the earth in silk shea - -
thing, in shim-me-ring trin-kets un-cea - -
sing, in shoes that are sound-less-ly trea - -
ding, for such is the Christ-child's own bid- ding.
Lyre ostinato

A Boy's Resolve

H. Ritter
Lyre
1. A Knight will I be-
2. Who shall be my ex-
3. He's o-ver-come the
come__ a war-rior strong and pure that
am-ple, whose arm is swift and strong? The
dra-gon, through cloud and smoke he's come. Let
to the good on earth___ the vic-to-ry be
im-age in my shield doth to Mi-cha-el be-
him be car-ried on--ward as war-rior of the
sure,
-long,
sun.
Lyre

St. Nicolas

M. Garff

Lyre prelude
1. From out the clou-dy height __ u-
-pon his char-ger white __ rides thun-de-ring to
earth a-gain Saint Ni-co-las, the ho-ly man.
2. While in the wood the hare ____
sniffs of the win-ter air, ____
the stag with his great horn ____
leaps o-ver bush and thorn. ____

3. And all the beasts a- bout ____
they quick-ly scam-per out ____
and glad-ly well-come here ____
the horse and ri- der dear. ____
4. A song we now will try ____ of
gol-den stars on high. __ We'll sing to him when
late he knocks at our gate.
Lyre postlude

Christmas

M. Tittmann

Lyre prelude
1. When the dain-ty snow-flake stars
2. Where the shep-herds through the night
3. When the songs of an-gels ring:
1. fall on lands all dark and wild
2. guard their lamb-kins small and mild
3. "Earth by God is un- -de- -filed",
1. mid- night bells chime near and far,
2. flow- ers bloom all sil- -ver white
3. shines the sun in hearts a- -gain,
1.2.3. mo- -ther rocks her lit- -tle child,
mo- -ther rocks her lit- -tle child.
Lyre postlude

Father Joseph's Hood

M. Garff

Lyre prelude
1. The
2. It
dain-ty, dow-ny flakes you see on
slum-bers un-der the green roof and
Fa--ther Jo--seph's hood. The
feels no wind or cold, while
ba-by 'neith the tall spruce-tree is
o-ver God's own son the woods their
warm in win-ter's wood.
si-lent vi-gil holds.
Lyre postlude

Dragonfly

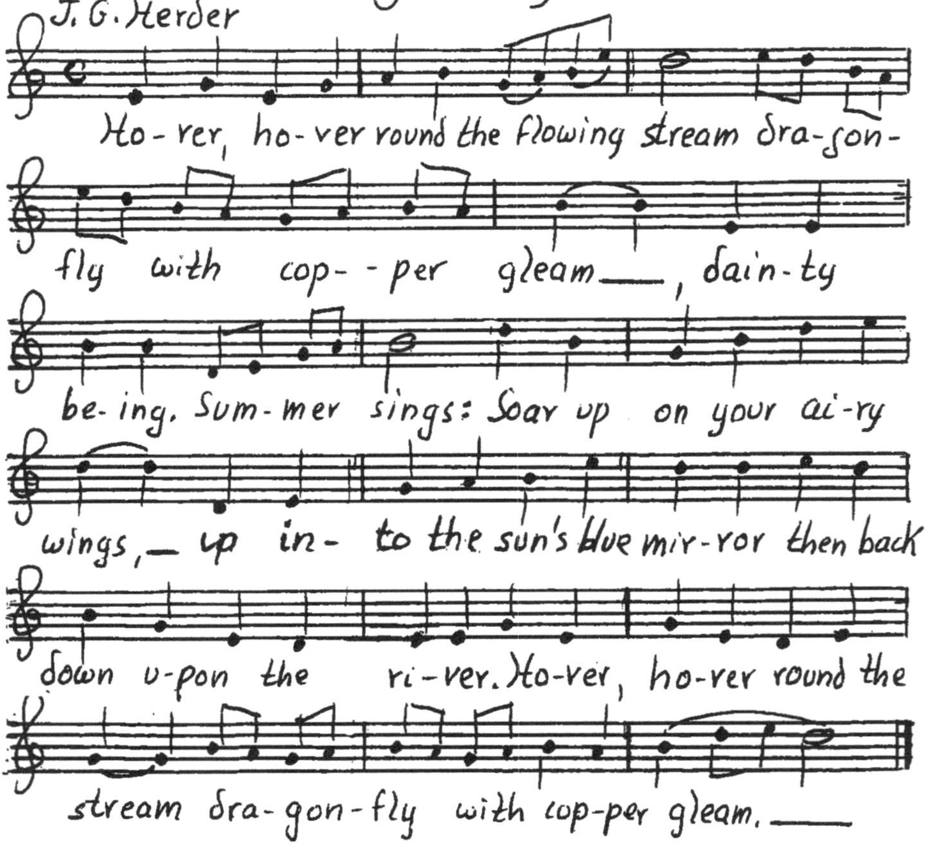
J. G. Herder
Ho-ver, ho-ver round the flowing stream dra-gon-
fly with cop--per gleam___, dain-ty
be-ing. Sum-mer sings: Soar up on your ai-ry
wings,_ up in- to the sun's blue mir-ror then back
down u-pon the ri-ver. Ho-ver, ho-ver round the
stream dra-gon-fly with cop-per gleam.___

The Trees Stand All in Flower

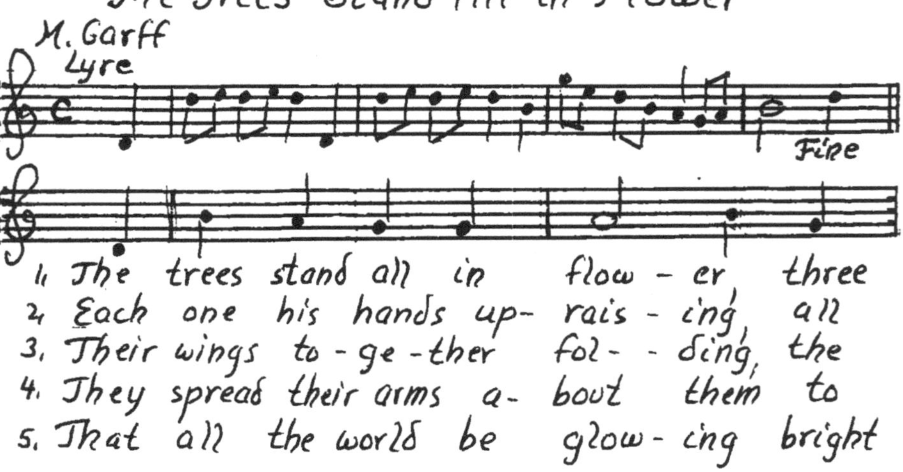
M. Garff
Lyre
Fine
1. The trees stand all in flow - er, three
2. Each one his hands up- rais - ing, all
3. Their wings to - ge - ther fol- - ding, the
4. They spread their arms a- bout them to
5. That all the world be glow - ing bright

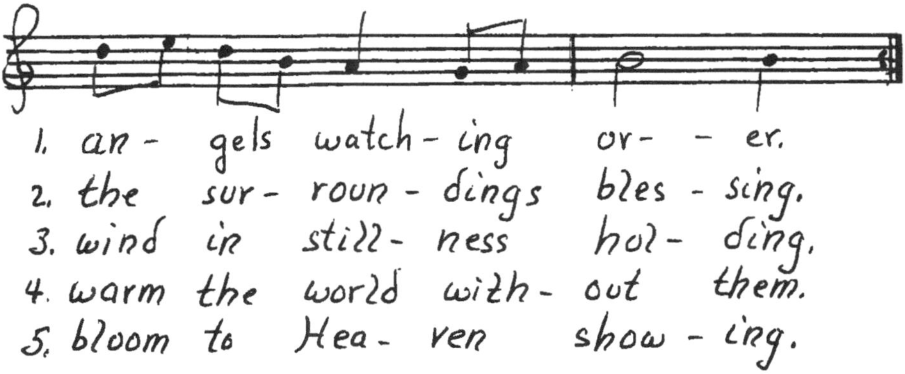
1. an- gels watch- ing ov- - er.
2. the sur- roun- dings bles - sing.
3. wind in still- ness hol- ding.
4. warm the world with- out them.
5. bloom to Hea- ven show - ing.

The Trout

M. Garff
Fla- - shing trout slip round a- bout with-
in your springs swim in and out.
Fine
The nix-es in_ the wa-ter-fall, they're
play-ing, play-ing ball, it bubbles and
foams, it sports and springs, it rings and sings:
Da capo al fine
Is this not fun? Oh run!_____

Tweet Tweet, Tweet

Marie Grandin

Lyre
Tweet, tweet, tweet,
Cui, cui, cui,
the bird is wa- king
l'oi seau s'é-veil- le
to the bright morning
aux clairs ray-ons du ma-
ray.
-tin,
Buzz, buzz, buzz, the
Bour, bour, bour, dé-
bee is ta- king
jà l'a beil- le
from the flow-ers
sur les fleurs prend
her sweet tea.
son bu - tin.
Tweet, tweet, tweet,
Cui, cui, cui,
buzz, buzz, buzz,
bour, bour, bour,
hm - - - - - - - .

Halloo, Hallay, I Feel so Gay

M. Garff

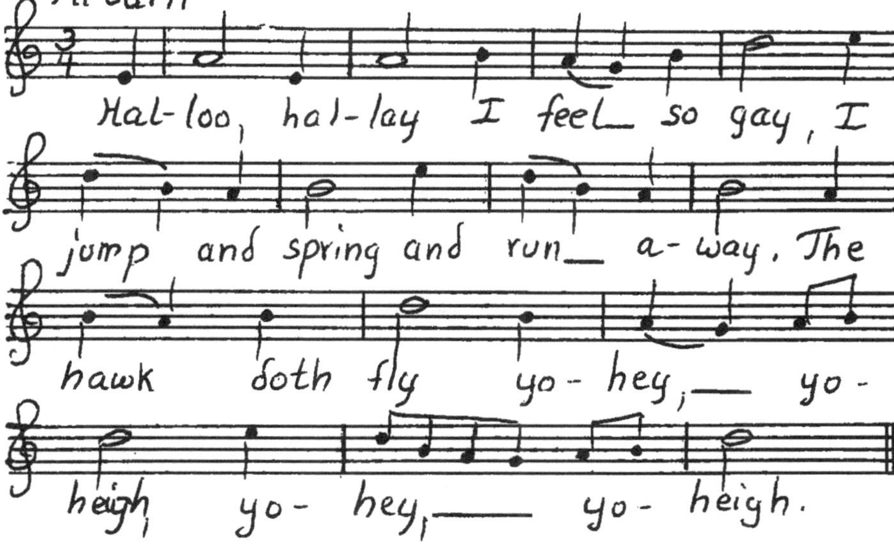
Hal-loo, hal-lay I feel so gay, I
jump and spring and run a-way. The
hawk doth fly yo-hey, yo-
heigh yo- hey, yo- heigh.

Butterfly Floats to and fro

M. Garff

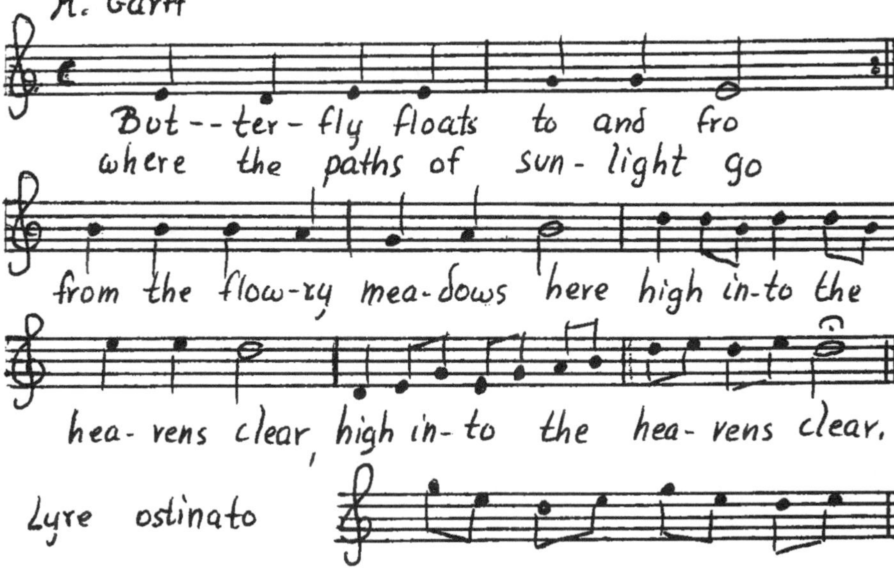
But--ter-fly floats to and fro
where the paths of sun-light go
from the flow-ry mea-dows here high in-to the
hea-vens clear, high in-to the hea-vens clear.
Lyre ostinato

Come Wind and Blow the Clouds

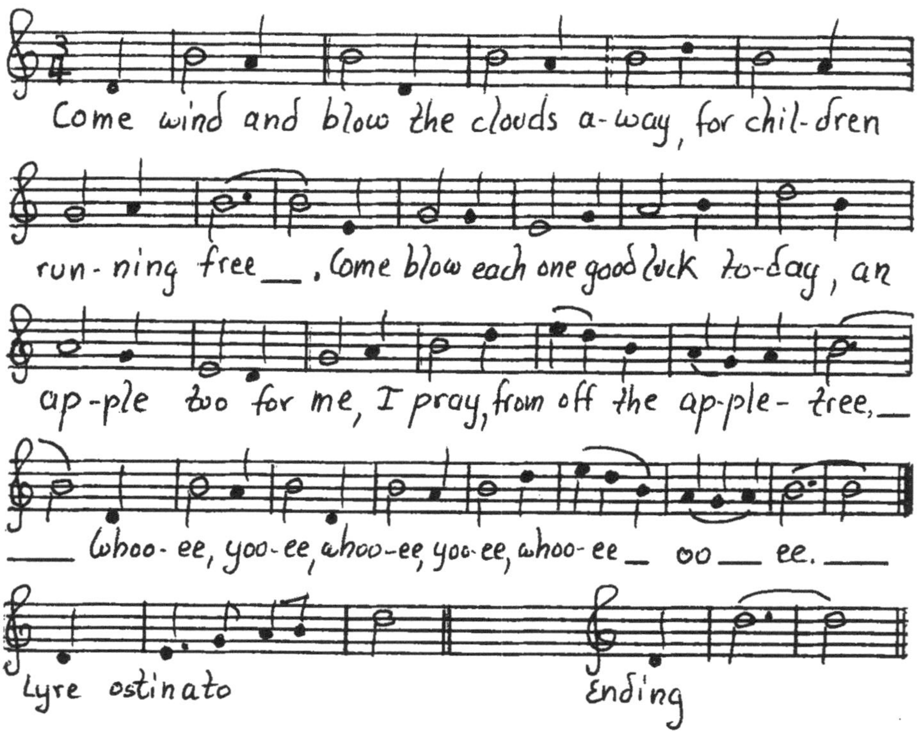
Come wind and blow the clouds a-way, for chil-dren
run-ning free__. Come blow each one good luck to-day, an
ap-ple too for me, I pray, from off the ap-ple- tree,__
__ Whoo-ee, yoo-ee, whoo-ee, yoo-ee, whoo-ee_ oo__ ee.__
Lyre ostinato
Ending

Butterfly

From "Bimbam Belletje" by H. IJzerman
1. Fly, fly, but-ter-fly___
2. Fly, fly, but-ter-fly with
Lyre

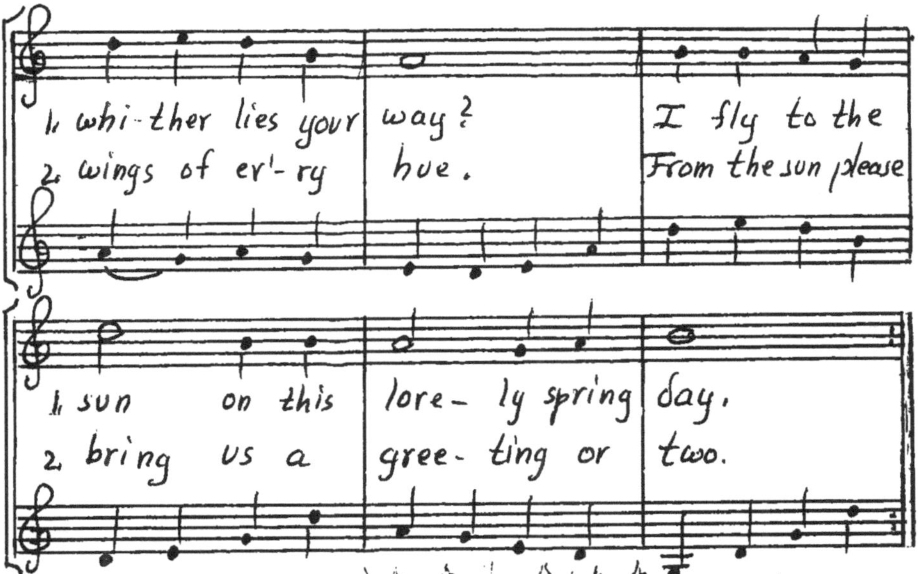
1. whi-ther lies your way? I fly to the sun on this love-ly spring day.
2. wings of ev'-ry hue. From the sun please bring us a gree-ting or two.

Hark, the Bells

M. Garff

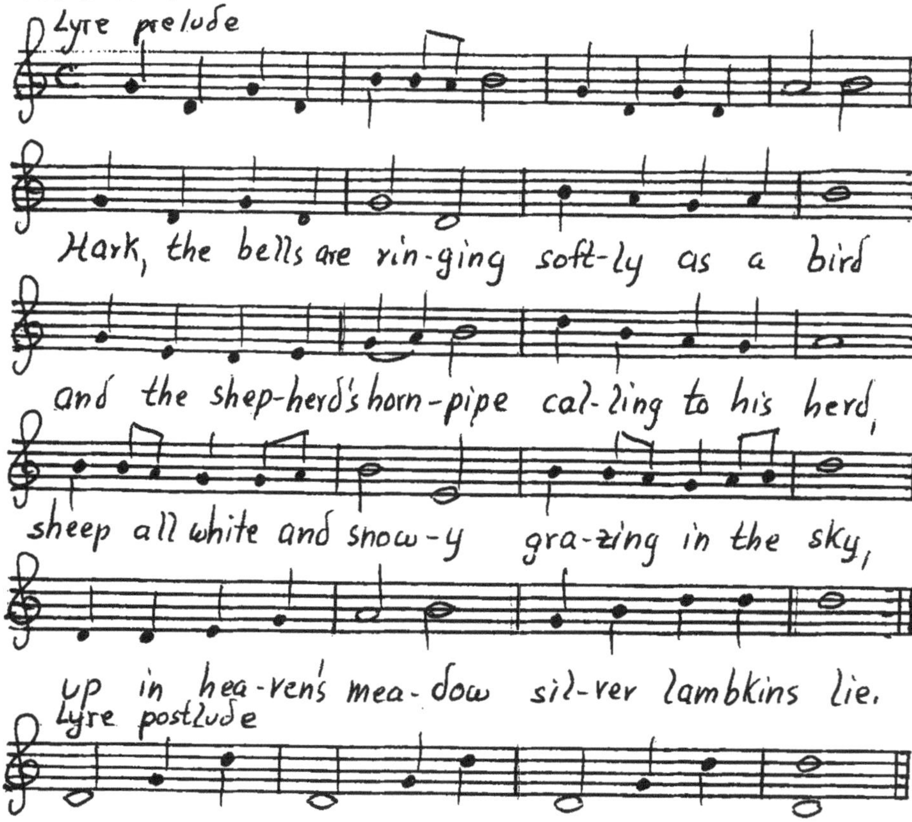
Lyre prelude
Hark, the bells are ringing softly as a bird
and the shepherd's horn-pipe calling to his herd,
sheep all white and snow-y grazing in the sky,
up in heaven's meadow silver lambkins lie.
Lyre postlude

ostinato to the song

The Apple

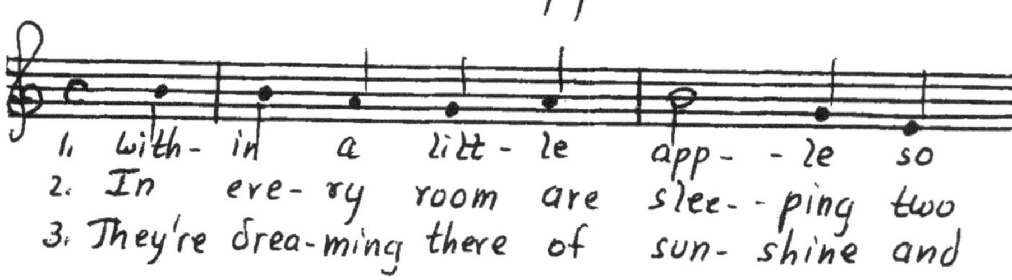
1. With- in a lit-tle app- - le so
2. In eve- ry room are slee- - ping two
3. They're drea-ming there of sun- shine and

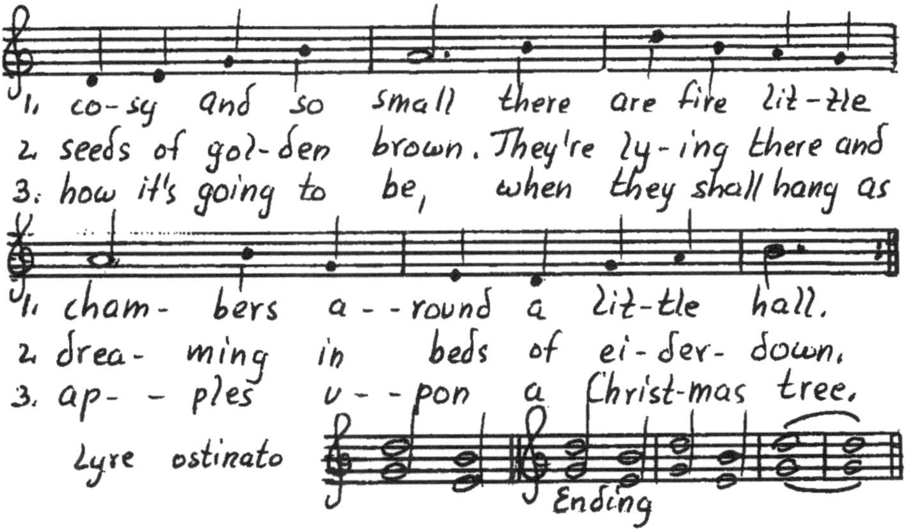
1. co-sy and so small there are five lit-tle
2. seeds of gol-den brown. They're ly-ing there and
3. how it's going to be, when they shall hang as
1. cham- bers a--round a lit-tle hall.
2. drea- ming in beds of ei-der- down.
3. ap- - ples u--pon a Christ-mas tree.
Lyre ostinato
Ending

The Brook

M. Garff

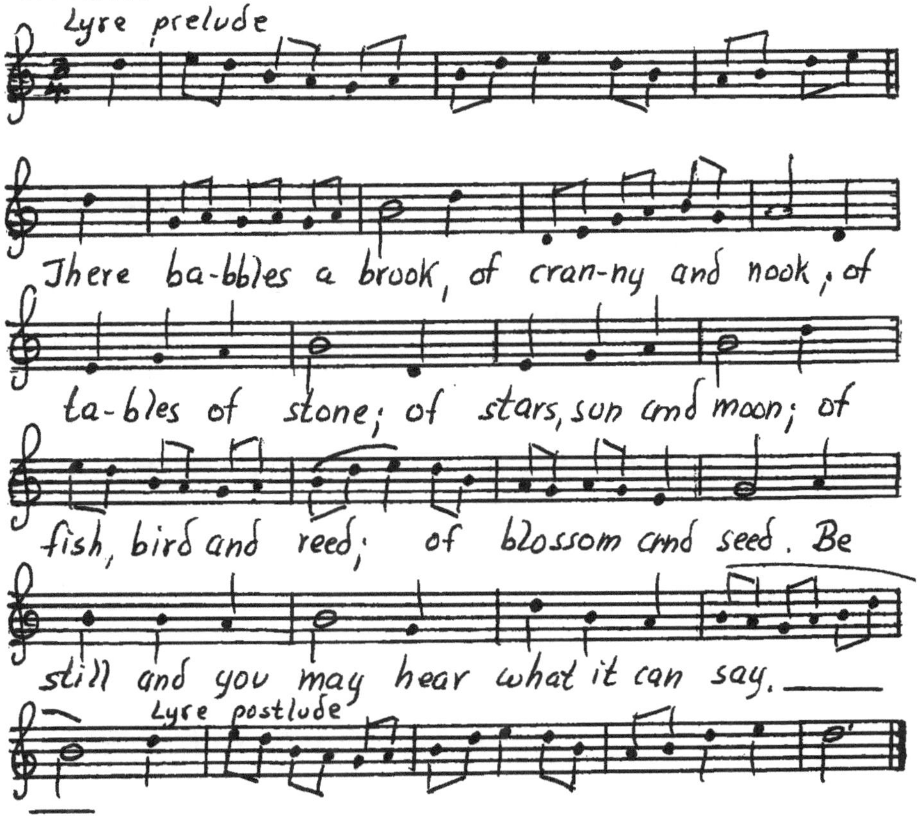
Lyre prelude
There ba-bbles a brook, of cran-ny and nook, of
ta-bles of stone; of stars, sun and moon; of
fish, bird and reed; of blossom and seed. Be
still and you may hear what it can say.
Lyre postlude

The Sea Is Deep

R. Hey
Lyre
The sea is deep, the sea is broad
and yet the glo - rious - ness of
God goes deeper than the sea's dark ground
is broa-der than the earth a- round.
Humm repeat.

Stirring Batter

Lyre prelude
M. Tittmann
1. Stir-ring bat-ter, stir-ring bat-ter, stir it so it
2. Stir-ring bat-ter, stir-ring bat-ter, taste a bit, it
3. Stir-ring bat-ter, stir-ring bat-ter, Sun-day din-ner
does not spat-ter. Round a-bout the
does not mat-ter. Mo-ther dear, please
makes you fat-ter. Young and old to-
bowl is right. White and gold and gold and white
show me, show is it sweet e-nough, the dough?
ge-ther eat, think that cake is such a treat,
winds it--self and finds it--self and
Just a__ nib-ble, taste a__ lit-tle,
makes you__ stron-ger, grows you__ lon-ger,
smooth and sti-cky binds it-self__. Pa-tient stir-ring
not to lick and not to quib-ble. Don't you see, I
it's the best to still your hun-ger. All our love and
makes the cake which the ba-kers-man can bake.
thought as much! Needs more su-gar, just a touch.
care we'll bake right in-to__ the yel-low cake.
Lyre postlude

To My Angel

M. Jittmann

1. An-gel, sent to me by God who my
2. Give to me new pow'r of life, glad-ly
1. hea-ven-ly ca-noe safe-ly
2. may my work full-fill so that
1. guides through world of stars, let me
2. bu--sy be my hand, steel and
1. glad-ly wake a-new.
2. streng-then well my will.
Lyre ostinato
Ending

Oh See How the Beech

M. Garff

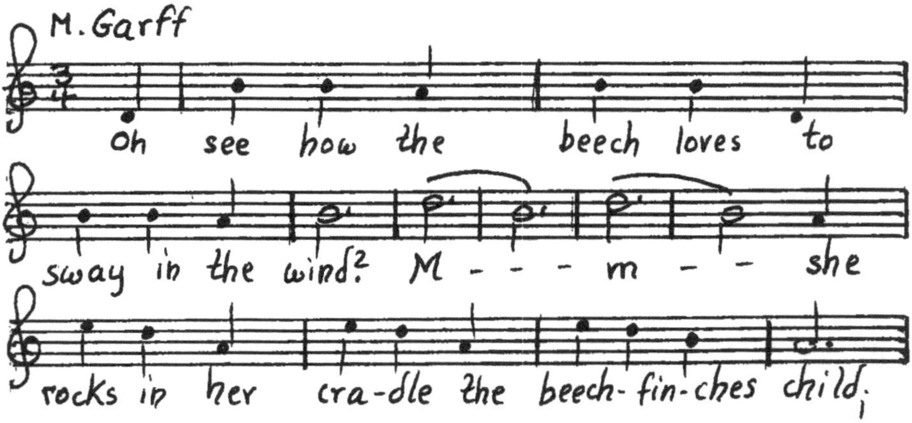
Oh see how the beech loves to
sway in the wind? M---m--she
rocks in her cra-dle the beech-fin-ches child,

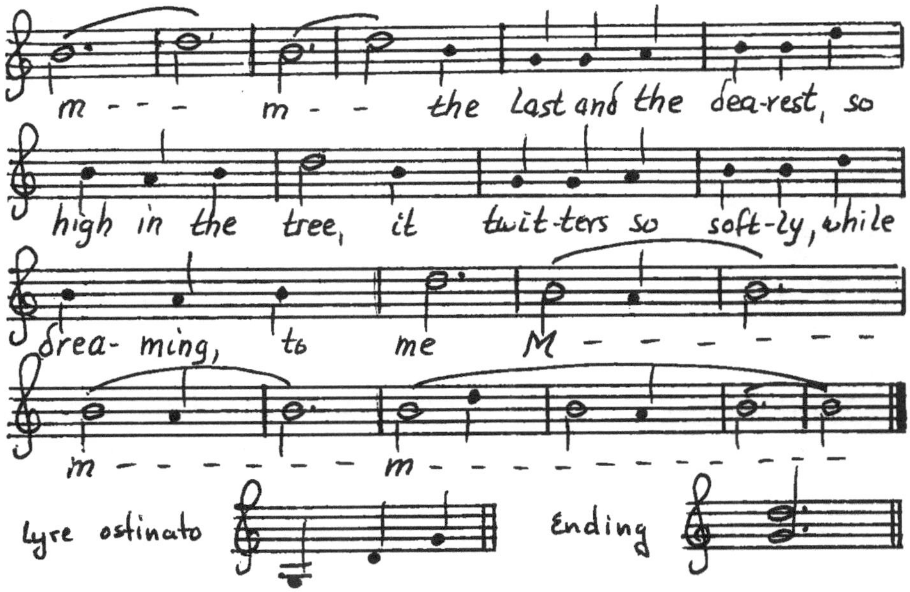
m - - - m - - the last and the dea-rest, so
high in the tree, it twit-ters so soft-ly, while
drea- ming, to me M - - - - - - - -
m - - - - - - - m - - - - - - - - - - - - -
Lyre ostinato
Ending

Lullaby from Island

For Ulrike Dorothea Wessel, 1957

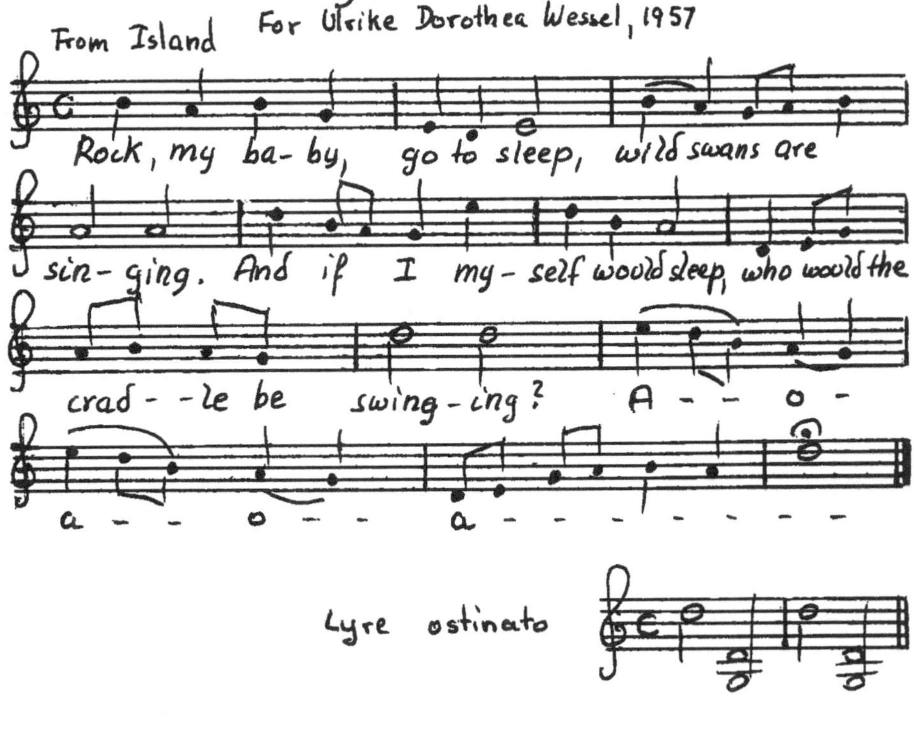
From Island
Rock, my ba- by, go to sleep, wild swans are
sin- ging. And if I my- self would sleep, who would the
crad- - le be swing- ing? A - - o -
a - - o - - - a - - - - - - - - -
Lyre ostinato

Dors Mon Petit Enfant

Sleep, litt - le ba - - by mine, sleep
Dors mon pe - tit en - fant, dors
in your cra-dle fine. Slum - ber soon will
dans ton lit tout blanc, som - meil bien-tôt va
come — a - gain, dear ba - - by close your
re — ve - nir, l'en - fant ché - ri — va
eye - lids then. Hush, hush my litt - le one,
s'en — dor - mir. Do - do pe - ti - - - - te,
hush, hush the day is done. Hm-
do - do bien vi - - - - - te. Do-
-m, Hm - m, Hm - - m - - m. —
-do, do - - do, do - - do - - do. —
Lyre ostinato

Bird's Cradle

A. Dieffenbach

Lyre
Soft - ly go - ing, soft - ly blow - ing through the
trees the wind is heard. Ei - a, ei - a
ei - a, i, soft and slow, to and fro
ro - - - cking the ba - by bird. Ei - a, ei - a,
ei - a, i, ei - a, ei - a, ei - a, i.

The Stars in the Evening

H. Diestel

The stars in the eve-ning now rise in the
blue, the blos-soms are cat-ching the sil-ve-ry
dew, the trees do not rust-le, the bu-shes are
still, and do-zing are e-ven the sheep on the
hill. Why keep you a-wake? You shall sleep ___, with
bu-shes and trees and the sheep ______, with
bu-shes and trees and the sheep ______.

Sleep, Baby, Sleep

From Holland

Sleep, ba-by sleep, out-side there stands a

sheep, a sheep stands with a spot-ted cow, my
ba- - by— close your eye-lids now.
Lyre ostinato

A Sound Rings Forth

M. Garff

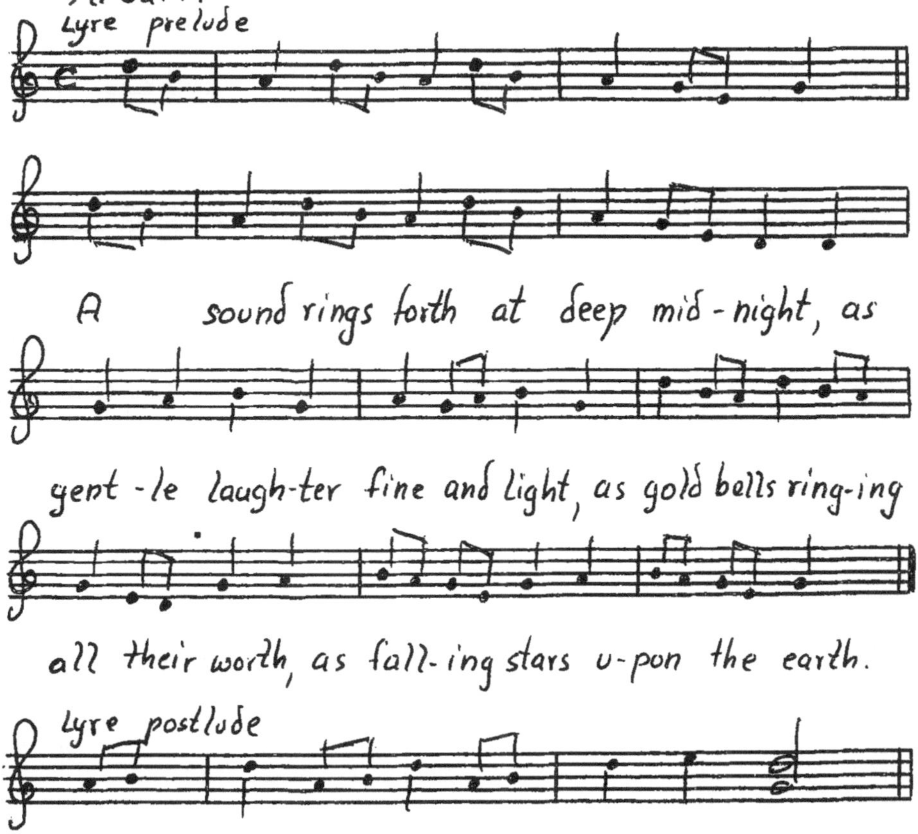
Lyre prelude
A sound rings forth at deep mid-night, as
gent-le laugh-ter fine and light, as gold bells ring-ing
all their worth, as fall-ing stars u-pon the earth.
Lyre postlude

Sandmen

H. Diestel

Lyre
We're coming from the moon's fair land with
lit-tle sacks of sil-very sand. We tip-toe to your
bed at night and then our sacks we o-pen wide.
Close your ti-red eyes now tight
and slum-ber sweet, my lit-tle child!

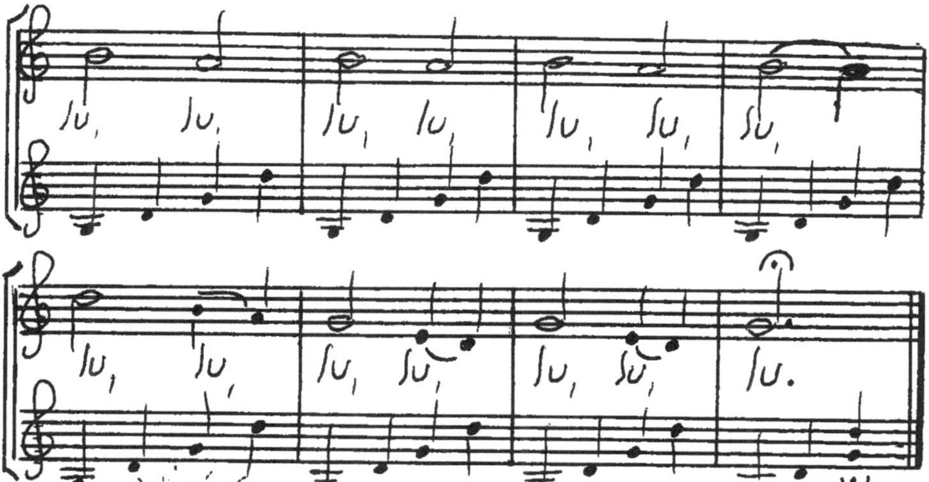
lu, lu, lu, lu, lu, lu, lu,
lu, lu, lu, lu, lu, lu, lu.

Bàyushki Bayù

From Russia

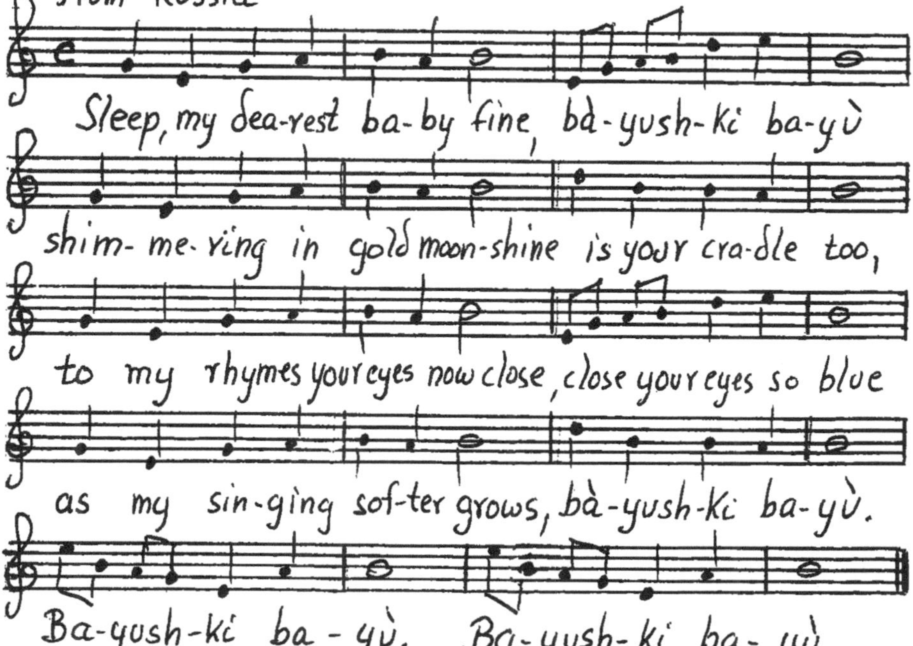
Sleep, my dea-rest ba-by fine, bà-yush-ki ba-yù
shim-me-ring in gold moon-shine is your cra-dle too,
to my rhymes your eyes now close, close your eyes so blue
as my sin-ging sof-ter grows, bà-yush-ki ba-yù.
Ba-yush-ki ba-yù. Ba-yush-ki ba-yù.

Lyre ostinato

Ending

Dream, Baby, Dream

Chr. Morgenstern

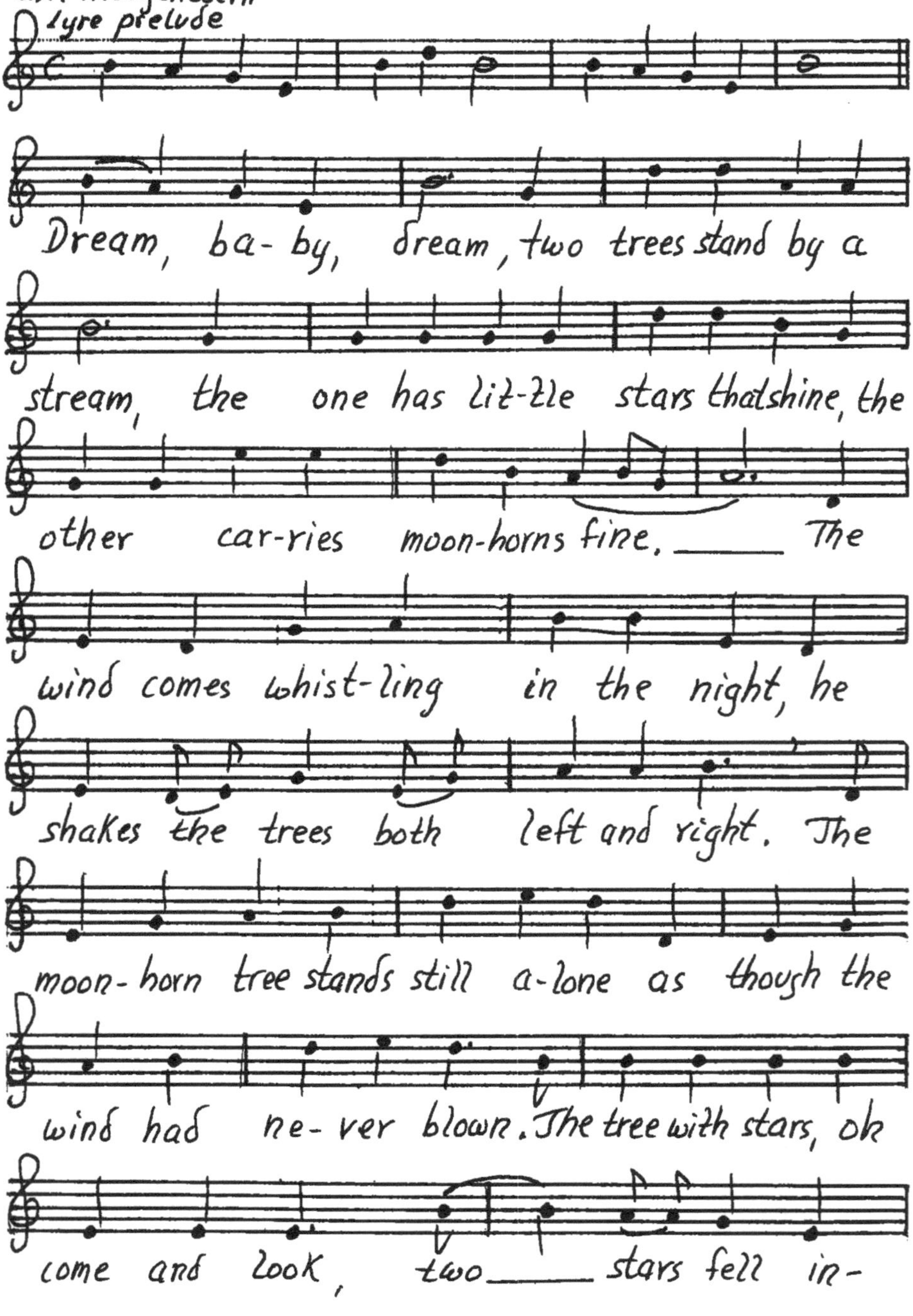
lyre prelude
Dream, ba- by, dream, two trees stand by a
stream, the one has lit-tle stars that shine, the
other car-ries moon-horns fine. The
wind comes whist-ling in the night, he
shakes the trees both left and right. The
moon- horn tree stands still a-lone as though the
wind had ne- ver blown. The tree with stars, oh
come and look, two stars fell in-

to the brook. Some fi- shes hur-ry round
and swal- low the stars right down
And if no stars had fal-len in, their
scales wouldn't shine like po- lished tin.
Dream, ba- by dream, two trees stand by a
stream, the one has stars that shine, the
o- ther car-ries moonhorns fine.
dream, ba- by, dream, dream ba- by
dream.

Lullaby from Finnland

Close_ your eyes__, my heart, my ba - by.
I__ will rock_ you, slum - ber sweet - ly,
sing__ un - til_ your eyes_ are drow - sy,
and__ in sleep's own sleigh will drive you.
Soft- - ly trea - ding come_ and vi - sit,
love- ly sleep, come take_ my dar - ling.
In your arms you'll hold him soft - ly,
in your sleigh you'll lay him safe - ly,
at your side you'll lay— him safe - ly,
Keep him safe from eve- ry dan - ger,
on the sof - test roads you'll drive him,
le- vel streets you'll choose to take him.

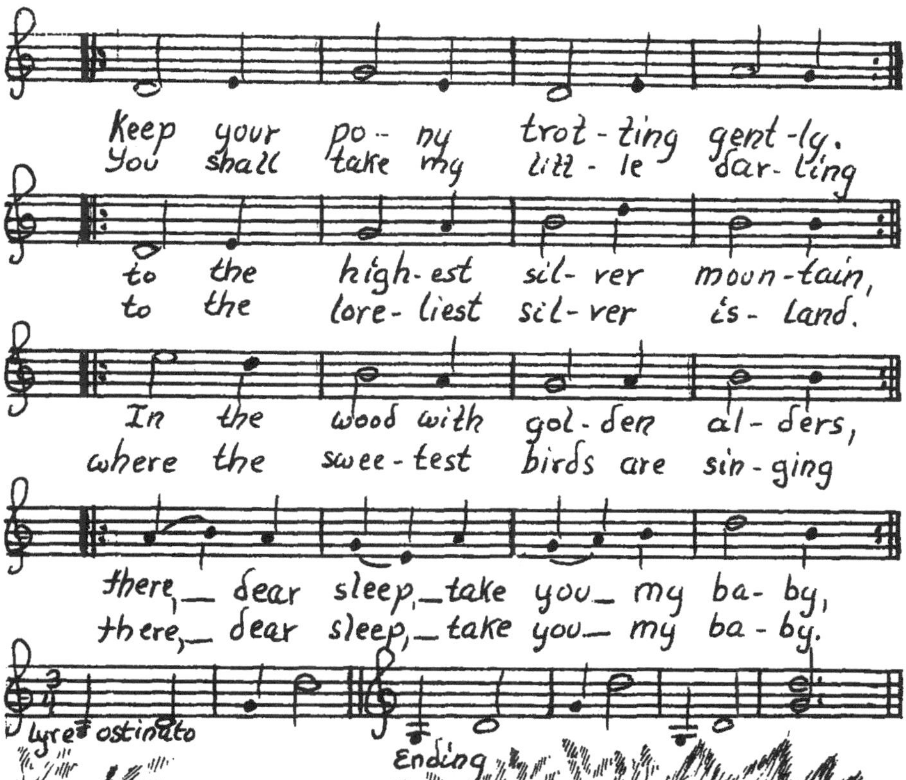
Keep your po-ny trot-ting gent-ly.
You shall take my lit-le dar-ling
to the high-est sil-ver moun-tain,
to the love-liest sil-ver is-land.
In the wood with gol-den al-ders,
where the swee-test birds are sin-ging
there,_ dear sleep,_ take you_ my ba-by,
there,_ dear sleep,_ take you_ my ba-by.
lyre ostinato
Ending